Touch Me

A Beginner's Guide to Massage

By: J. A. Carlton
Massage Therapist
AMTA Member

Chapter 1 - Introduction

The intention of this book

After nearly twenty years as a massage therapist there are usually two questions I'm asked by the clients on my table, "Can you teach my husband/wife how to do this?" and "How can I do this for my partner?" usually with a telling smile in their voice.

So, after hearing these questions over and over again I decided to put my *mumbles an obscure number* years of experience as a writer to use for my career as a Massage Therapist and put together some very basic information about the human body, and about massage.

The main purpose in these pages is not just to provide the Anatomical and Physiological information necessary (bony prominences, main muscle groups etc) for the lay person to give a good massage to someone they love; but also to give a little insight into how the giver can and does effect the receiver, and how to make it an optimal experience for all parties concerned.

Massage is essentially educated and practiced rubbing. Everyone has their own unique rhythm and sense of motion that feels right to them.

What I hope to accomplish here is to help those who are interested, to cultivate their own unique massage style while providing valuable anatomic and technical knowledge that will reduce the likelihood of discomfort or injury. The information will also help both the giver and the recipient get a better "feel" for their body and nurture a deeper, more satisfying relationship between both parties whether the relationship is platonic or more intimate.

There is no information contained in this book that is meant to be construed as medically diagnostic, nor will the information provide the reader or lay-practitioner with any kind of expertise that is a replacement for proper education in the way of Massage or the Healing Arts.

All the information contained herein, as well as the philosophies and theories posed are relayed strictly for the purpose of enhancing interpersonal relationships without fear of causing harm.

How the information is applied to your individual life, or your relationships with your loved ones, is completely up to you.

One quick note... please keep your nails trim and smooth, it'll be more comfortable for both of you.

Matter:

For our intents and purposes here Matter is any solid object that can be touched.

Energy:

Can neither be created nor destroyed, and is essentially (in the world of quantum physics at least) the most basic building block of EVERYTHING, *even matter.*

The Energy of Touch:

Believe it or not, it's about more than the weight of someone's hand on you. My clients are often more aware of how I feel about a particular project or endeavor before I'm aware of it myself.

Some of them have cited a change in pressure as the giveaway, others the speed or type of stroke, or even the depth and length of time I may linger on any given trigger point as the most telling factor.

The point is that something going on inside my head and heart is being communicated through TOUCH to my clients, many of whom are friends as well.

Oddly enough though, these same cues have also been cited as the telling factors when my mind is on something that's troubling. But what's really interesting is the way the difference has been described even if the technique is the same; often as a sense that I'm 'cut off' or 'not really there'.

To every one of my clients and friends who understands how essential communication is, I am grateful for those times you bring me back to YOU. Thank You.

Touching is first and most obviously a physical connection, but second and even more importantly it is an *emotional* connection.

In our bodies we hold tension in certain places.

An adult who was sexually abused at any time, or made to feel ashamed of their body in any way may hold tremendous tension in their legs for instance, their muscles rock hard and immovable as if they're forever ready to sprint away or escape. It's important to be aware that these 'holding' places can be any muscle or group in the human body, and that it is possible that by working on that area, you might elicit an emotional release from your partner, sometimes it'll be a strong one that may make them cry, or laugh, or even tighten up further if they're not ready to deal with it, and sometimes it's as simple as a sigh.

If your partner tightens up while you're working on them, it's not advisable to ask them if they're having an 'emo' moment, you can and should however ask them if you're hurting them, or if they'd like you to stop what you're doing, and act accordingly to either adjust your pressure and/or technique.

Mindfulness when giving massage is essential and has its own section in chapter 3. It's a small but very important detail that can mean the difference between a positive experience and a ho-hum or even negative one.

Chapter 2 - Basic Massage Strokes

(a Brief Overview)

But first! A wee bit of history:

What is massage? Simply put, Massage = touch (usually with rhythm).

From the dawn of life on this planet, every living thing responds to SOME kind of touch, including the touch of energy itself.

Plants respond to actual physical contact and the energy that comes from that contact, as well as solar and wind energy.

Flowers are pollinated in part due to contact with other living entities, bees, hummingbirds, bats, bugs, etc. As well as by the caress of a gentle breeze that carries the pollen to other flowers.

Animals, especially social animals groom each other to establish bonds, to reinforce the social order or hierarchy of the pack, pride, pod or family. They touch to give and receive comfort, to show empathy, to nurture, to improve health and lower stress levels, to lend strength and emotional support. And of course they touch to mate.

Make no mistake, just because we can rationalize doesn't mean we can live without touch.

This is your chance to give something of yourself without hesitation or reservation to someone you care about. From platonic friendships to our most intimate lovers, touch is truly a profound means of communication. You most certainly know people who have difficulty verbalizing feelings of love, trust, caring or intimacy, but have no compunction about dropping a reassuring hand on your shoulder. When they do that, you feel your shoulders fall, you feel some of your stress abate, you *feel* what their energy is saying even if it's something their words cannot.

Massage and touching is instinctive. No one can claim ownership to it, no one can claim to have started it and no one can claim to have discovered it. It is also one of the areas of life in which the effects of the mere act of *thinking*, manifests almost immediately, translated through energy, motion, and depth at the very least.

There are numerous techniques, styles and methods: Swedish, Deep Tissue, Myofacial Release, Shiatsu, Reflexology, Acupressure, Reiki, Feldenkrais, Orthobionomy, Cranial Sacral and a plethora of variations on these techniques. Every one of them was started, developed, devised, patented and packaged by someone at some time.

But not massage. It belongs to every one and every thing. To touch someone is natural, whether it is a good thing or a bad thing depends entirely on the INTENT.

For decades studies have been done on how physical touch can affect health. Premature babies when massaged gently grow and put on weight roughly twice as fast as those who are not touched in other than a clinical fashion. Many nurses and NICU (Neonatal Intensive Care Unit) staff often learn neonatal massage to help nurture underweight babies.

At the other end of the spectrum geriatric patients (a tragically HUGELY ignored population in American culture), often report feeling a noticeable reduction in the every day aches and pains associated with arthritic conditions and muscle fatigue. They've also noted an increased sense of well being and contentment once touch is introduced back into their daily lives.

So, if you're lucky enough to have a senior citizen that you love in your life, give 'em a hug, give 'em a cuddle, give 'em a kiss and tell 'em you love 'em, and remember they loved YOU first. And if they're not the cuddling, hugging, kissing kind... scratch all that and respect their boundaries and tell 'em you love 'em. Kindness carries its own energy.

At First

This new way of touching may feel awkward, both to you and your recipient. Working on peers; brothers, sisters, friends, is always different then say working on a parent or grandparent especially if you're going to be working with bare skin and oils verses a "tune-up" through clothing.

If this is a new experience for the recipient its possible there may be some giggling, laughing, ticklishness and guarding going on when you first lay your hands on them.

If it's giggling and laughing, it might be wise to ask if you're tickling them, it may just be that you need to use a slightly firmer, and flat hand. Fingertips are often associated with tickling especially when the touch is a little lighter. The use of your whole hand, say on the back between the shoulder blade and the spine is a good place to start to get your recipient accustomed to your presence.

Of course, this doesn't mean slapping your hand down on the person, just laying your hand on them, usually in a benign place like the shoulder or the upper back (the lower back is inherently a more intimate place to touch than the upper so before you move down there... "introduce" yourself, your touch and your intention in a place less likely to be guarded like the upper back.) let your fingers relax and contour to the skin, muscle and around the bony prominences. Once contact has been made and accepted (about a breath's worth of time) you can start to move slowly and with fairly firm pressure, almost as if you're beginning to spread bread dough.

Alright enough preaching, let's move on to some of the basics.

Two of the most commonly used strokes in your standard Swedish style massage are called Effleurage and Petrissage. These are also the two most common ways the average individual massages their partner even without having any technical education.

Many friends and clients smile just a little wryly when they talk about how little time their usual massage partner is able to spend working on an area before they claim they're too tired or their hands hurt.

If all you're using is your hands and forearm muscles it's no wonder. One of the secrets to being able to give a fair massage for a decent duration is to use a little bit of your body weight as leverage. What I'm talking about here is instead of using just the muscle of your hands to obtain any kind of 'depth', try leaning in just a little bit and letting some weight help your hands (usually the heel of your hand just between the palm and the wrists) sink into the muscle. Try this for a few minutes and see if both you and your partner don't notice a little bit of a difference. It's not about strength, it's about leverage.

The motion of your strokes should come from the shoulder rather than just the hands. We've all had someone who when they've tried to rub our shoulders simply feels like they're pinching. Well, that's most likely exactly what they're doing. When a motion comes more from the elbow and shoulder it tends to be a little more rocking and rhythmic, and a lot more soothing.

For the largest purpose of this book we're talking about working on your partner either on a massage table, firm bed or the floor, some place the recipient can comfortably lay down and let you work their stresses away.

Effleurage

Draping: fold the sheet down to the recipients' waist exposing the back, neck and shoulders; gently rock their hips back and forth a little to anchor the sheet under them.

Effleurage strokes are more surface oriented and tend to be used for warming. It is a light to moderate push/pull stroke usually done with a relaxed open hand. The movement is hand-over-hand with moderate speed and depending on the depth and heat desired can start in the fingertips, run down the pads of the fingers to the ball and then the heel of the hand making sure to use all the fleshy parts.

Start with a quarter sized squirt of oil, warm it between your hands, and standing at the head of the table place your hands at the shoulders and slide gently down the center of the back (one hand on either side of the spine, *not* directly on the spine itself) toward the top of the buttocks. Once there spread your hands a little wider on their back as you draw them up again. Do this move a few times, not only is it a good way to get that nice starting layer of oil on the back, but it's also a great and easy way to get both of you into the right mindset by introducing skin on skin touch.

When warming the surface with effleurage, it's recommended that the push be directed toward the heart when working on extremities, if you're using this stroke on the back, either moving toward the sacrum, or up toward the shoulders is perfectly, perfect. When working more deeply and using more 'strip' like strokes especially on the limbs, again, try to make sure that you're draining or pushing toward the trunk of the body.

The veins in the legs have valves that angle upwards to help combat the effects of gravity, the most healthful way to move fluids through the body is toward the heart. Many massage therapists will use a light effleurage technique that may move from the trunk downward toward the toes for instance, this is not wrong necessarily but neither is it optimal. If someone uses a lighter technique pushing toward your toes, it's most likely for variation and you shouldn't necessarily worry about it unless it makes you (as the recipient) feel uncomfortable.

Petrissage

Petrissage is a somewhat deeper technique, this is the one that's more like kneading bread-dough. It incorporates properties of both effleurage and some lighter myofacial techniques like skin rolling and gentle kneading to help increase blood flow to an area. Both of these techniques help oxygenate tissues by spreading muscle fibers and breaking up adhesions (gummy spots) where muscle and connective tissues may have become stuck together.

The surface of the skin should move with some moderate independence from the musculature beneath. Everyone knows someone who feels as if their body is made of stone (not just because they're muscular) because their skin and their muscles aren't capable of moving independently.

For example, place a fingertip on your forearm and gently try to move the skin toward your elbow, if the surface of the skin moves a few millimeters with ease, then it's a fair bet that you're not particularly adhered in that spot.

Petrissage can be done by either grasping the muscle between the thumb and fingers (gently of course you're not trying to pinch here) or curling your hand around the muscles to slightly raise and knead them.

Trigger Points

Trigger points are small clusters of cells within the muscle that when touched tend to refer pain to a different area or simply radiate it to a larger part of the same area.

For instance, one might have a trigger point in the layers of muscle between the scapula and the spine that will refer a pain up into the neck or shoulder.

Your partner/recipient (just to be clear I'm using the word 'partner' here in the sense of someone that you're going to be exchanging massages with, not necessarily in a sexual sense), will help you identify trigger points.

Usually they're found in the muscle stripping stage of effleurage massage work since they do tend to exist on a deeper level in the body. Sometimes the recipient will gasp, or tighten up, or somehow twitch to indicate that you've hit a 'spot'. From there, it's just a matter of finding the center of the spot itself and gently trying to coax it to release.

Trigger points can be treated with relative ease and with far less pressure than you'd think. (We've all seen videos, skits, gags, etc where a 'therapist' breaks out a hammer and chisel, jackhammer, or some such nonsense... well trigger points can be difficult but sheesh! Anyway, leave the heavy duty tool use to the professionals please, you're here to nurture, we'll handle the Therapy). If the trigger point doesn't release with a little steady pressure, say 3 ten second 'holds', then you may have to face that it's just not ready to let go.

If you find one on your partner or recipient, gently place the tip of your forefinger on the center of it and press into it slowly increasing the pressure. In order to preserve and stabilize the joints of your forefinger, simply cross your middle finger over the forefinger and brace the distal phalanx (the part with the nail) with the pad of the middle finger. This will provide extra joint stability as well as a bit more depth.

-        When working with a trigger point please be sure to check in frequently with your recipient. "How's this?"

"Is it too much pressure?" "Is it referring?" "Where to?" etc. and note the responses with more than just the words. Are they gasping for air? Are they whimpering? Grunting? Groaning? Slapping the table and kicking their feet?

-        If so you might want to back off just a bit.

Once you're certain you're in the center of the trigger point and that it's 'active', hold your pressure for 10 to 30 seconds.

Repeat this 'activate and hold' three times; each time, if necessary with a gentle reminder for your partner to take a nice deep breath to help bring fresh blood and oxygen to the area.

There are a lot of areas in the body that can cultivate trigger points, the most common are in the shoulders; on the back between the shoulder blades and the spine, and up in the back of the neck, along the path of a muscle called Levator Scapula.

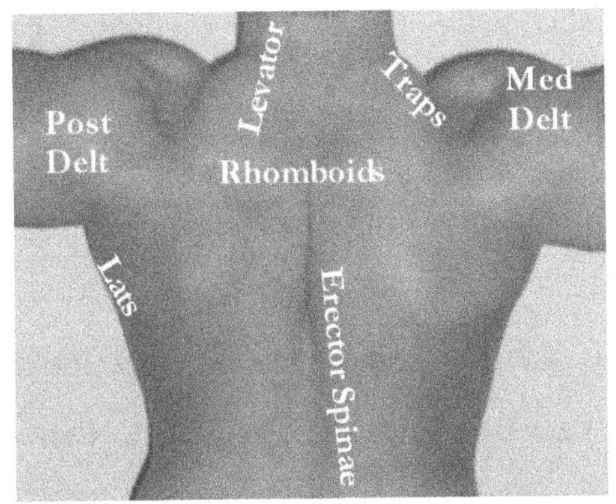

Levator
Traps
Med
Delt
Post
Delt
Rhomboids
Lats
Erector Spinae

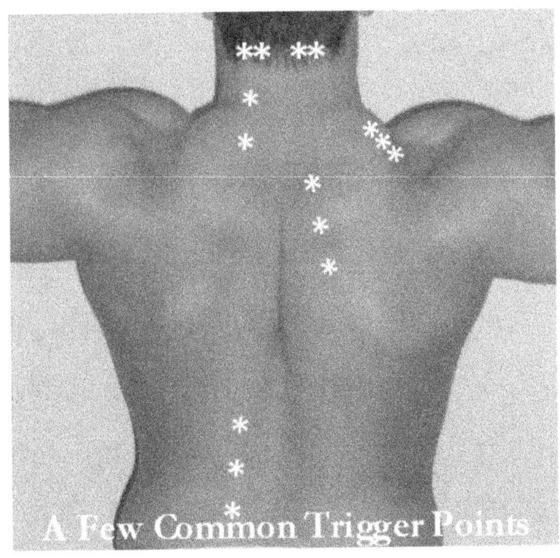

A Few Common Trigger Points

Knots

Knots are just what they sound like. Knots are bundles of muscles that are 'knotted' or twisted up.

Knots are typically very easy to identify. They're the 'lump' in the mashed potato of your musculature. Fingers tend to want to hop over or press into them as you massage your partner, usually on the back and the tops of the shoulders. Knots can be handled the same way as trigger points, and also with a combination of effleurage and petrissage strokes.

What IS a "knot"?

Usually they're bulky bits of muscle that have formed for any number of reasons, sometimes they stem from over-stretching. Very much like a rubber band that has been stretched too far too fast and winds up curling up on itself. The same thing can happen to muscles if they're stretched too cold, too fast.

There's been some debate and as many opinions as there are people, about whether or not warming a muscle before stretching it really makes a difference. My personal opinion is, Yes, it matters. You won't get a good stretch and you may do more harm than good if the muscle isn't warm before you stretch it. It just makes sense.

Just think about mozzarella sticks. When they're room temperature they break with relative ease, but when they're hot they stretch much better. Or remember when you were a kid and stuck a piece of already chewed gum into the freezer on a hot summer day, then when it was frozen you tried to stretch it and it snapped? Well the gum example may be a little extreme but the concept is the same. A cold muscle will be more traumatized by sudden stretching than a warmed one will be. Also a warmed muscle will be full of fresh blood and oxygen, enabling it to maintain its nourishment WHILE you're working it.

Knots are also, no matter HOW they are formed, comprised of traumatized tissue.

Going back to the 'cold gum' idea, when you start to stretch that gum and the edges of it start to fray and break down, the same thing can and does frequently happen to muscle. It's not a bad thing, this is how body builders BUILD their muscles, with layer over layer of muscle tissue and fibers that have been broken down and rebuilt to compensate for increased usage. What can make this process less than optimal is when regular movement and flushing to the area is lacking (i.e. exercise), and the frayed material doesn't get flushed away but instead accumulates inhibiting movement, oxygenation, possibly nerve conduction and decreasing overall health and performance.

Then there's lactic acid build-up. These are the knots that burn sometimes when you're breaking them down for your partner. Often they're confused with trigger points because they're very painful, however remember that a trigger point *refers* pain to a *different* location than where it's palpated. This is your main means of distinguishing one from the other.

Often time lactic acid build-up happens from a lack of stretching and proper hydration, although in many cases it is also caused in part from working out/building muscles in areas that are hard to stretch such as the rhomboids, (a deeper set of muscles between the scapula and the spine).

No matter what caused your knots, working out, or work itself (think the static position held for hours on end while you work on your computer for example), bringing fresh blood and oxygen to any knotted area with the use of massage will provide relief and enrich the depth of your connection with your recipient and he or she with you.

Light Myofacial Release Techniques

Segmental Stretching and Skin rolling are the two primary types of myofacial release strokes that I'm going to address here. They're really all that should be necessary in the home setting.

Skin Rolling

This is honestly one of my least favorite modes of achieving myofacial release. No matter how careful the practitioner is, it often pinches and then burns, even though it's only for a few minutes. It is without a doubt an extremely effective means of separating the layers; skin, connective tissue, and muscle from one another, but there are other ways to do this that are more appropriate for the non-professional.

Still, skin rolling is done by grasping a segment of skin between the thumb and fingertips and lifting the skin slightly. Once you have the equivalent of a hot dog between your fingertips and thumb; rock your thumb and the skin against it toward your fingertips. Once you've gone as far as you can with the 'hot dog' still firmly held, walk your fingertips another inch or so away and repeat the process through the area.

If your professional uses this technique on you, the odds are you really really need it, and their use is far more therapeutically oriented than yours should be when working with your partner.

Remember you're here to nurture and as one of my clients frequently admonishes, "For God's sake don't ever show my wife how to do this! When I need torture I'll come to you!" And he does.

Segmental Stretching

This is a far less painful though sometimes not as therapeutically effective means of performing myofacial release.

This is however a means that can benefit you both tremendously by providing a gentler way to loosen muscles, adhered tissues and decease pain by increasing oxygenation and blood flow.

Segmental stretching is done once the surface is adequately warmed, one of the most common areas to use this technique is on longer muscles or groups, such as the Erector Spinae, literally 'Erect Spine'; these are the muscles that can be easily felt immediately to the left and right of the spine itself that travel from the base of the skull all the way down to the hips. These are some of the hardest working muscles in the human body aside from the heart and the piriformis (we'll get to THAT one later!).

Perform this type of stretch usually with the first two to three finger tips. Follow the length of the muscle until you reach a particularly tight spot, gently allow the finger tips to sink into that spot until you feel like you have a gentle hook-type grip on the muscle rather than just the skin (with a little practice believe me you'll know the difference), and gently draw the muscle back toward you by about an inch.

Please be aware of the length of your fingernails, both men and women... please make sure they are trim and without jagged edges, flaying is not what we're after.

This technique is usually used, again on the muscles along the spine, but if you try to use it somewhere else, say the rhomboids you should be aware that you may be spreading muscle fibers on an angle to how they run in the body. There's no harm in doing segmental stretching this way, it's just something you should be aware of.

There are less frequently used techniques like Tapotment, jostling and certain deeper types of friction which are best left to your professional to do.

Tapotment is the light tapping of the fingertips or percussion (kinda like drumming with a loose hand) on the muscles (not over the bony areas please).

Jostling is an easy, gentle shaking of usually a limb or a larger muscle or group (hamstrings, quadriceps, biceps etc). Sometimes your partner will tighten up without realizing they're doing it, particularly if you've hit a tender spot, a little jostle to the area will help the muscles to loosen again.

When to Go Deep, and How Deep do I Go?

Since your purpose here is to nurture and not necessarily therapeutic, you're really not going to be working terribly deeply on your partner, but you do want your touch to be felt and to communicate your caring intent.

This is where verbal communication and intent begin to truly enter the picture. Your partner is asking you for something, is it to work out a knot? Is it pure stress reduction? Is it a nice little combination of both?

Even on clients I've worked with for years, whose thresholds and tolerances I know better than my own; when I'm working with active intent on a particular spot, when I'm working deep, I check in (i.e. "Is this okay? Is it too much? You want me to back off?") perhaps too much but better too frequently than not enough.

You may know or have a massage therapist who frequently uses their elbows on your toughest places, this is where I strongly suggest that you *leave the elbow work to your properly trained professional.* For this reason I'm not going to cover therapeutic Deep Tissue techniques.

At this stage of the game you want to stick with fingertip pressure, loose fist or even some light knuckle muscle stripping, or trigger point manipulation.

Just because you want to give of yourself to your massage partner doesn't mean that you should ignore your own body signals. Please be careful with your fingers, more of us use our hands (usually for computer work) on a daily basis and with more constancy than ever before in history so please treat your self with just as much respect and care as you do your partner.

Chapter 3 – Intent is Everything

Determining the Purpose of your Massage

I've already addressed your intent in giving the massage so far, but your partner also needs to have an intention in mind.

Are they there to relax? Are they on the table/floor/bed grudgingly or to placate you? Do they WANT to unload their stress at this moment? Are they looking to get aroused? Is this a precursor to foreplay? To sex? To some other form of entertainment?

What is it that you BOTH are intending to get out of the *giving* and *receiving* of this massage?

Whatever the purpose is, it is without a doubt imperative for both parties to agree on the intent and have fairly clear boundaries that need to be considered pretty darned sacrosanct, (the exception being a massage between lovers who later agree on altering the intention and desired outcome. It's a fact, if you're working with or on your significant other, the mood *can* change when the stress starts to retreat).

The only way both parties are going to be able to adequately determine the purpose of the massage is to communicate. Talk, sign, write notes, emails (I'd suggest keeping that kind of thing at home though), make an appointment with each other, set aside the time. Just COMMUNIATE, it's as easy and as dauntingly difficult as that.

Men rarely have any difficulties communicating what they need in a business sense, in an exercise sense, in a financial sense or even in a dating or relationship sense. They usually have a SOLID idea or vision. When it comes to receiving massage though (thankfully this is getting to be less and less frequently the case in the clinical setting) sometimes guys are less inclined to admit that they have pain or discomfort anywhere.

Ladies when your man asks you to massage him (for the purpose of pain relief) understand he's letting you in on the human inside the hero that he wants to be for you.

Women on the other hand, are known to be more in tune with their bodies and what's going on inside them at any given time. Unfortunately, in part thanks to the woman's rush, push, desire to prove their equality in the business world, many have learned to ignore every day aches and pains much the way men have, until issues become physically limiting or even debilitating. This is most likely due to the fact the most women still carry the insane notion that it's more important to put someone else's needs over their own. (Can we STOP that please? Men know it, we should too... we can't take care of anyone until we learn to take care of ourselves! *breathes* okay I'm done).

Men, when your woman asks you to massage her (for the purpose of stress relief), understand she's giving you the opportunity to let your inner hero shine.

And if your significant other happens to be the same gender as you, well then, you've probably established your roles already so ... pick one of the above and apply it to whomever it belongs.

Mindfulness

Mindfulness is simply keeping your mind and your focus in the here and now, on what you're doing, and on your partner.

One of the nicest things about getting into a rhythm when doing a massage is that it can be a very meditative process for the practitioner, it can reduce YOUR stress level, it gives your mind a chance to let go of some of the trials and tribulations of the day.

Unfortunately, it can also sometimes lead to the minor irritants (or major ones) of the day circling your head over and over again. If you're anxious, believe me your partner WILL feel it.

This is your opportunity to clear your mind, to focus on the tactile sensation under your fingertips, knuckles, palms whatever part you're using. It's your chance to change the focus, to turn your mind away from your problems and focus on someone else's well being. This change in focus will come home to you as your mind begins to let go of external irritants and seek its own balm in the sharing of energies and the communication of caring and the desire to cultivate wellness within someone you care about.

Communication is Key

This is your and your partner's chance to really think about and improve the way in which you communicate. And it's a chance to refine the nature of, and your interpretation of constructive criticism.

For instance, perhaps the first clue you've hit a tender spot in your partner is a gasp. Maybe that gasp is accompanied by a flinch, or an "Ouch!" If so, this is the time for you as the practitioner to ask, "Is it too much? Do you want me to back off?"

You might be surprised that sometimes your partner will say "No. It's okay keep going." This is especially true if your *intention* is to HELP.

If however you're having a bad day and doing the work grudgingly, your partner will most likely feel your antipathy and may well say, "Yeah, a little."

Effective communication is really the only way to even begin to give or receive a massage.

If you're a recipient and you're flopping down on the table just to appease your partner, and you're really not in the mood to get a massage (I'm having difficulty imagining that), it might not be the right time. Perhaps you need a little time to unwind after a long day, or to let go of some of the rough edges before you let anyone into your energy; this is the time to communicate that need. You can do that by making an appointment.

For instance:

You lost an account you've been working with for months, you had a feeling they were going to go with someone else but you still gave it your best shot. You walk into the house/apartment feeling defeated and more than just a little like you've been road hauled.

Your partner chirps a happy greeting and immediately tries to steer you to the massage table, "I know JUST what you need! C'mon lay down..."

But you just know that every touch is gonna sting, you're not in the mood, the wound is too fresh.

IT'S OKAY!

It might be difficult to be sensitive at this moment, but try to be as you say, "Gimme a half hour to shake off the day..."

Boom, you've just set an appointment.

Now it's your partner's responsibility to understand that you're *not* rejecting *them*, **OR** their attempt to give you relief or comfort, but in order to optimize the experience you have shake off the crap.

You don't hop in the shower without taking off your clothes; likewise, sometimes you can't enjoy a massage until you've discharged some of your inner static.

The important thing to remember so you can react from the most considerate place possible is to remember your partner's *INTENTION*.

We've been so thoroughly trained in the art of the witty comeback, the stinging barb, the dig to someone else in order to make ourselves feel better that we often use these devices against the very people we rely on to bring us comfort at the end of the day.

Chapter 4 – Body Components

For our purposes here we're going to go with the most well known layers of the body.

Starting at the most superficial (surface) we have skin. Skin is the largest organ of the body. It breathes, it is semi-permeable, it grows and changes. The primary function of the skin is to protect the organism (you) as a whole, from everything from 'the elements' to ambient radiation.

To this end you might ask, then why is it so sensitive? The long and short answer is simply to keep us from damaging ourselves, in particular through carelessness.

Next we have fat, the depth and quantity of which varies from individual to individual.

Then we have connective tissue, just like the milky little membrane over a chicken breast when you skin it.

The fourth layer we're concerned with is the muscle layer, this is where we store most of our tension and our responses to day life, both good and bad. (The indifferent really doesn't hang around).

The next parts we're concerned about are the bones. Certain bones can be felt, and sometimes seen very close to the surface of the skin; the acromion process of your shoulder, the scapulae (your wings), clavicle (collar bone), elbow etc. One of the reasons these areas are so important is because locating and palpating (feeling) them will help you trace the paths of the muscles nearby.

All these things from skin to muscle to bone are there to protect your internal organs, most of which sit in the thoracic, abdominal, and pelvic cavities. Natch your brain gets its own special carrying case.

Just so you know, the skeleton is usually considered in two segments:

The Axial – which are all the bones of your trunk basically; head, vertebrae, ribs and pelvis (all those parts that protect the inside organs that make you, YOU.).

And The Appendicular – comprised of your shoulder girdle, arms, and legs, (all the parts that SERVE you.).

Chapter 5 – Body Regions; Trunk, Arms, Legs.

This section will contain the bulk of the anatomic information you're going to need to give a good massage to someone without hurting them.

Here we'll cover the major bony landmarks in each region of the body, the nearby major muscle groups and some techniques for massaging each region.

For our purposes here we're going to presume that your partner will be at least partially disrobed and modestly covered with a top sheet unless otherwise noted. We're also going to presume that oil of some kind will be used to facilitate the process and prevent friction burns.

A quick word about oil application; more oil = more slickness, less warming and the possibility of bumping into a bony prominence with painful (for both or either of you) results.

It is best to err on the side of moderation; enough oil to get some good glide over the skin without losing control, but not so much that you can't build up some good warmth in the muscles.

Of course, you can always dab some of the excess off too or apply more as needed.

Alright then, as they say in music, let's take it from the top:

Introducing Your Touch

Whether your partner is clothed, or draped makes no difference here. The first thing you want to do is to "introduce yourself" to their space. Your introductory touch will establish the intention of the massage and convey to your partner just how comfortable you're going to be in this new endeavor.

Working through Clothing: If you decide that even partial undraping is too awkward, at least at this stage of your relationship you can easily still give a massage, you can still indulge in your nurturing self and still begin the process of cultivating a new level to your relationship.

The only difference is that you'll be doing away with most hand-over-hand longitudinal gliding strokes. Kneading, knot work, trigger point work, and segmental stretching can all be done on a clothed partner. Your technique is as adaptable as you are, and if you find something that works but isn't listed here, by all means, as long as it's comfortable for you both, use it. This is only a guide, all the rest is you and your partner. Just as it should be.

The best introductory touch is when your partner is lying on their stomach. For this one you should be standing at the side of the table, with one hand between the shoulder blades and the other in the small of the back, gently rest your hands on their body, feel free to rock your partner a little this often helps to dispel the last of whatever stressors might be blanketing them at the moment, (fresh stressors from their day) and opens the way energetically for deeper communication.

Continue this for a couple deep breaths, both of you taking the opportunity to center yourselves and get in tune with each others' energy.

Once you feel centered and able to focus your attention properly on your partner, you're ready to begin giving your massage.

The proper beginning of any massage is an assessment, and this is where self knowledge comes in very handy. You know *your* tight spots, go ahead and use your fingertips, gently prodding (not poking), the upper shoulders, that area between the shoulder blades, the muscles on the sides of the spine. What you're looking for here is resistance or resilience, mobility, does it feel like a rock? Like cold clay? Does it move? These things alone will tell you some of the most troublesome areas your partner has that need to be worked.

Every time I start with a new client or someone who isn't very experienced in receiving massages it is inevitable that they ask, "How can you tell the difference between a regular muscle and a tight spot?"

The only answer that seems to make any sense is the following idea. If you were to take several sections of garden hose and lay them side by side, and among them you placed a piece of lead pipe the same diameter. Even if your eyes were closed and you had mittens on (very much like feeling muscles beneath skin), you'd still be able to tell which was hose and which was pipe. If you're paying attention to what you're doing and what you're feeling, you just know.

52

So now that you know your partner's tighter areas, those that are going to need a little extra attention you can start your massage.

Shoulders and Upper Back

Draping: If your client is laying down on a table or bed and has chosen to allow you to work on them without a shirt or bra on, there should at least be a sheet draped over them.

At this point, fold the sheet down to the hips exposing the whole of the back down to the dimples just above the buttocks. If they're wearing underwear you can tuck the sheet a bit into the waistband to prevent oil from getting into the garment. Next gently rock your partner side to side while easing the sheet under the front of their hips to hold it in place.

If your partner is seated or has elected not to disrobe at all then there's no need for a sheet 'cause you won't be using oil.

If your partner is laying down and disrobed and if you are using oil, start with a quarter sized squirt of some kind of jojoba, coconut, or genuine massage oil. Warm the dollop between your hands and from the head of the table, or bed with a firm glide spread the oil from shoulders down to the sacrum, starting on either side of the spine, and as you return toward the neck drawing your hands up the outer sides of the torso, over the shoulders and up the neck to the base of the skull.

Repeat this application move a few times to give yourself a chance to sense the texture of your partner's body and muscles, to find their 'hard' or 'knotty' spots and to figure out what is bone and what isn't if you don't already know. Repetition of this move also gives your partner a chance to get accustomed to having someone's hands on their body in a non-sexual capacity.

The most common areas to hold tension and feel the effects of today's lifestyles are in the shoulders, upper back and neck. Almost everybody loves a good shoulder squeeze! (the primary muscles here are the Upper Trapezius or upper traps). Unfortunately lots of times what should be a squeeze is actually a pinch.

One of the ways to avoid pinching the upper traps or really any muscle group, is gently lay your hands on your partner's shoulders (this one is most commonly done while sitting), and curl your fingers (like they were inside mittens) over to the other side, in this case, over the tops of the shoulders. As you're folding your hand over the muscle group, gently push forward and slightly upward with the heel of your hand. (The fleshy part located just under your thumb).

You don't need a lot of force to do this and by using your fingers to brace the movement, instead of being the source of it, you won't get tired so quickly. Also your forearms won't fatigue because you're using leverage and just a little bit of body weight rather than muscle strength to do the job.

Your partner will appreciate the fact that you're not pinching and will be able to relax a lot more quickly and thoroughly and will be more willing to reciprocate, and that's what it's all about.

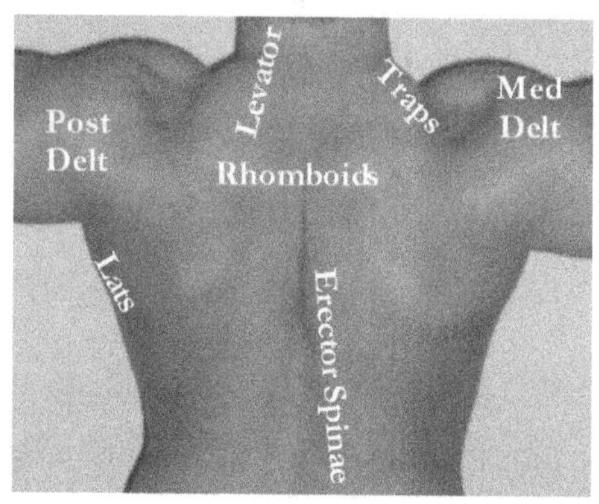

Post
Delt
Levator
Traps
Med
Delt
Rhomboids
Lats
Erector Spinae

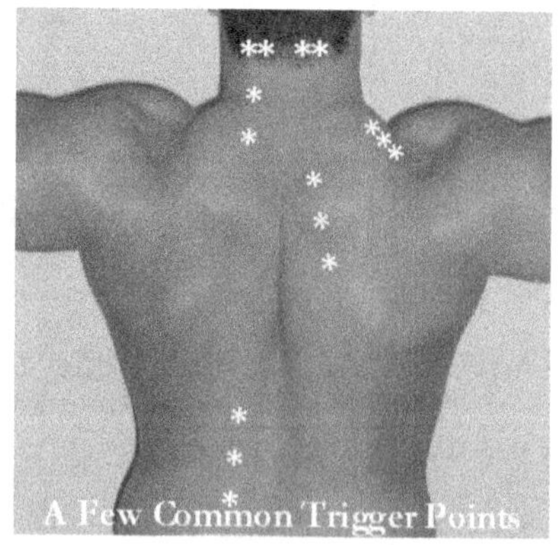

A Few Common Trigger Points

Arms (posterior aspect)

Draping: Maintain previous.

The posterior aspect of the upper arm is home to the triceps and posterior deltoids, and Teres major and minor (the muscles of the back wall of the arm pit).

On this aspect of the forearm you'll mostly find the flexors (the muscles and tendons that allow you to make a fist, or type or give you the strength to grasp things).

Warm and apply your oil with broad, firm but gentle strokes, this area can be very ticklish and highly sensitive, if approached inappropriately which usually amounts to being "addressed" too lightly.

The nice thing about working the arms is that the girth of it often fits within a two handed grip, allowing kneading of both posterior and anterior muscles.

When you get down to the forearm light muscle stripping from the wrist to the elbow can be hugely rewarding when most of the average person's work and recreational time is spent on computers or playing video games. Make no mistake however, crafters and artisans of all stripe from bricklayers to carpenters, any profession that relies on the hands for a final outcome (wouldn't that be just about every profession?) can almost certainly benefit from a little forearm t.l.c.

It doesn't take but a couple minutes, 3-5 to work the arm from the fingertips, (a little gentle range of motion here) to the palms (some light muscle stripping toward the wrist), and all the way up to the shoulder and back to the upper back to integrate the limb with the rest of the trunk.

Neck

Next we have the Neck. (Yes I know the neck is actually first in order from top to bottom but... it just makes sense to start with the shoulders. Besides, it's all connected anyway.) And here's why:

Along the sides of the posterior (back) of the neck are a couple muscles called Levator Scapula. There's one on either side, each one attaches to the upper inner border of your scapula (the wing), travels upward alongside the cervical (neck) vertebral column and ends at the base of your skull.

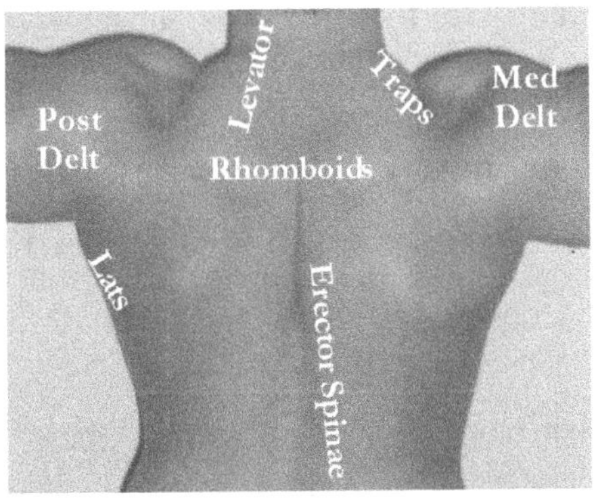

This is where you feel it when your neck is stiff at the end of the day from being on the computer for 10 hours, or driving for an obscene length of time in unending traffic. When your hand flies to the back of your neck and starts to squeeze it is almost certainly these muscles (sometimes they feel like bands of steel) that you wind up working. And when it's been an exceptionally rough day and you're feeling that tight, over-wound feeling in between your shoulder blades, it often started with these muscles tightening.

Levator Scapula and upper traps bear the horrific burden of being the ones that have to compensate for, and reflect the state of your life's stresses.

IF you choose to work your partner's neck while they're in a seated position, I'd suggest doing this at a table or desk where you can have them lean forward, resting their forehead on their arms or braced against their hands to give you easy access to their neck.

OR, use your own hand against their forehead to brace their head while you work their neck with the other hand. (If you use this method, make sure they're just resting their head against your hand and that you're not putting reciprocal pressure on the front of their skull).

The best technique for working the neck is a kneading stroke whether one handed or two it's between you and you partner. Usually knead with one hand first then the other, (rather than kneading with both at the same time) and you'll find your own innate rhythm.

The neck does NOT need a lot of pressure and one of the most important things to remember is that you're working the muscles on the SIDES of the vertebral column, NOT working the vertebra themselves. Please take care to make sure you are NOT working the center of the back of the neck.

You also want to make sure that you're not working the actual 'side' of the neck (as in lateral-most aspect of it). There are vessels here, [arteries and veins] that you don't want to put pressure on.

As for working too close to the spinous processes or the spine itself, a good rule of thumb is: IF IT FEELS LIKE A BONE, IT PROBABLY IS SO STOP AND MOVE OFF OF IT.

While you're working any group of muscles you may find knobby, knotty or crunchy spots and your partner may want you to dig into them.

In the neck I would suggest the use of fingertip pressure only, or at the very most and if you're well practiced, perhaps working or applying static pressure in that spot with a knuckle. This is done by simply sinking your fingertip or knuckle into whatever knot or crunchy spot you're working and once you've sunk into it, gently push outward from its center, usually up and down, but if you must then a very subtle side to side type 'sink' can be used to spread the fibers. Doing this slowly is more relaxing than doing it quickly, so please take that into consideration as well, after all you're not trying to nuggie the spot.

Speaking of nuggies, here's a variation that CAN be enjoyed. Once you've removed your finger or knuckle from the knot a nice little fingertip jostling (lightly place the pad of your finger over the area and give it a little wiggle.) can help relieve the sense of your finger being there and allows your partner to recover that much more quickly.

So now that you've finished sinking into the knots up and down both posterior sides of the neck, finish off with a minute or two of easy broad stroke kneading before sliding your hands down to the shoulders/upper traps again and giving them another minute or two of kneading.

The human body is a system of levers and pulleys, with muscles layering over each other.

When you've finished working each particular area, like the neck and shoulders; because of all the other muscles that surround it, a nice way to finish is with a flowing integrative stroke over the whole area that 'ties' it all together. It's like the sigh after a bout of belly laughter.

The Upper and Mid Back

Draping: Maintain previous.

Remember, any time you feel you need to reapply a little oil, go for it. Most genuine massage oils these days are pressed and formulated to be able to wash out of sheets, or you can just save a particular set of sheets for massaging on.

Here we're going to pay attention to the area between the scapulae, back up over the tops of the shoulders and even to the base of the rib cage.

Between the scapulae are three major muscle groups you're going to be concerned with, the erector spinae (which run along side the spine all the way from the base of the low back up to the base of the skull). The rhomboids which are the muscles used when you squeeze your shoulder blades together and Traps Two, or the lower aspect of the Trapezius muscles.

Most of the massaging you do along the back will most likely be length-wise along the spine, once again, please be mindful and do NOT work the spine directly.

The bulk of the erector spinae can be felt typically about a half inch to an inch and a half lateral on either side of the spine itself, and can sometimes feel like steel cables. Because of the width of these particular muscles, if you try to work them with a single finger or even two, you'll find in some cases that they're so tight they'll actually 'throw' your fingers off of them. Point is you just can't get a good grip. But don't give up, simply change your strategy. Try bracing the fingertips of your hands on either side of the muscles (again making sure not to put direct pressure on the spine) and use the thumbs to 'strip' the muscles.

OR if that doesn't feel comfortable, you can use the heel of your hand for a little more broad type glide over them. The biggest benefit of using a broader part of your hand to stroke the muscle is that your partner will be less likely to be ticklish, or to fight your intention. A broader surface contact is less likely to put someone physically on the defensive.

One of the things it's most important to remember when working on someone else is to understand how YOU like to be touched. How do YOU feel when someone pokes or jabs a finger into one of your knots? Do YOU find it easier to relax when someone uses a broader stroke on your shoulders?

If you're not sure how any of these things feel, then go ahead and TRY some of the different moves on yourself. You have tight spots, you have stiff areas, practice grabbing your forearm with 'mitten hands' then see if you feel the difference against the 'lobster claw' grip. See for yourself which one feels more inviting, warming and relaxing.

If you're not sure how much pressure to use when working a knot, practice on yourself. See how much YOU feel is beneficial for some of YOUR spots... it doesn't usually take more than just a few pounds of pressure to get the job done well and in a nurturing way.

The most important part of all of this to remember is your intent. Your intent here is to NURTURE your friends, your family, your relationships, your partner and through them even yourself. It's NOT a contest to see who can take the most pressure and it's not a contest to see who can get the most knots worked out or how quickly. It's about building a new level of communication between two people, one based on respect, mindfulness and active caring.

The Low Back

Draping: Maintain previous.

The low back is the harbor for almost all the end effects of stress in your life and world. For all of its strength and its lifetime of servitude to the body's rest and motion, it is an area that occasionally requires care and more than just a little bit of respect.

The previously mentioned erector spinae run the length of the low back, tapering off just above the sacrum (the flat part of your lowest back just above your butt) and aside from your obliques (the muscles under the love handles) are pretty much the only muscles you need to concern yourself with down here.

The low back also tends to have less fat than other areas of the body so it's important to remember that if you're working a little more deeply elsewhere, you might want to lighten up down here.

Now as you move down the low back toward the top of the butt you may notice a couple of dimples and you may feel a couple of fat pads around the area there. Please DO NOT try to work them out, they're supposed to be there. They protect the bones as well as the nerves that emerge in those areas to travel down the legs.

The low back is a good place for light thumb over thumb 'muscle stripping', and light heel-of-the-hand long strokes, the purpose of which should be the idea of decompressing the low spine.

The sacrum provides a perfect hand hold for a gentle lean against it. You don't want to bounce or 'pulse' down here, just some easy, sustained pressure, say for the span of 2 or 3 breaths can provide wondrous relief for an aching back after warming the surrounding muscles. And as you're working the back it's something you can go back to again and again as the muscles are warmed more and more effectively, until you're finished with the area and are ready to move on to the limbs.

Ribs

Draping: Maintain previous.

If your partner is lying down and not too ticklish, there are muscles between the ribs called Intercostal muscles that rarely get much attention at all. There is a wonderful easy technique for working saying a quick 'hello' to this particular area.

We all know what ribs feel like, so while your partner is laying on their stomach, start off by placing your fingers lightly directly on the rib cage, once you've found the bones, move either up or down so that your fingertips are now off them and resting in the spaces between. Feel how the ribs slant downward as they curl around the front of the body.

Go ahead and gently curl your fingers (flat-ish rather than hooked) around the torso in between the ribs. You should be standing on the left if you're working on the right side and vise versa when the time comes. Easily draw your hands around your partner's body toward the spine. Try this a few times on both sides up and down the rib cage, it's a surprisingly potent stress reliever.

Now that you've finished with the posterior torso, please cover your partner with the sheet as it is possible and probable that if you don't they may begin to feel cold as the heat you generated in their muscles dissipates.

Butt (draping)

Yes, I'm gonna explain a few things about the butt, yours, your partner's, and pretty much everyone whose got one so go ahead and let those giggles out, this is the perfect moment for it.

Done? Good.

Moving on now.

Draping: At this point you're going to fold the sheet over one entire leg back enough to expose the outer part of the hip on that side as well. Once you have the desired area exposed you can secure part of the sheet under the front of the hip near the waist line at the top, then making certain to dip fingers below the opposite leg (so you don't accidentally pinch the flesh there), anchor the inner part of the sheet there. Apply manually warmed oil along the entire leg from the ankle up to and over the hip. A good guide for exposure is a standard panty or underwear line to start with.

Okay when I say butt I'm not talking about the vertical smile, (save that for when you're playing with your romantic partner.) I'm actually talking about the posterior musculature of the pelvis which forms the cheeks. That would be the Glutes; Maximus, Medius, and Minimus, and Piriformis (the hardest working little muscle in the human body aside from the heart, at least in my humble opinion.) thankfully you don't need to worry about Piriformis. Let your therapist work on that fellah.

The pelvis is the source of stability in your body, it is your center of gravity and if the muscles that surround and work from it are either too weak or too tight, the rest of the body suffers.

Consider this area your axis for moving through the world.

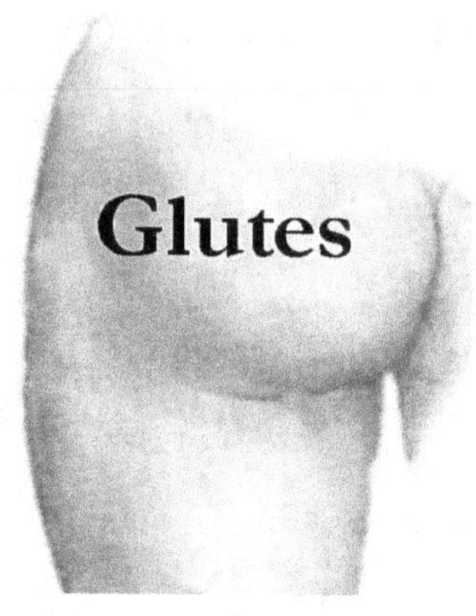

Glutes

As previously mentioned your skeleton is considered in two segments, one of them is the axial, and that consists in part, of your spine and pelvis.

It has been my personal experience that almost every muscular ailment that did not originate with either pathology or external mechanical interference (like whiplash for instance) can be traced to either hypertonicity (chronic extra tightness) or hypotonic (under developed) muscles surrounding and or attached to the pelvis. Some of these muscles are your 'Core' muscles (Abs, erector spinae, obliques, hip flexors etc) and some are more surface oriented like Gluteus Maximus. Still others are support muscles or those that have attachments at parts of the pelvis like your hamstrings, and quadriceps.

As I said before, the human body is a system of levers and pulleys, and everything IS connected.

So keeping that in mind if your hammies are hypertonic (too tight) and your quads are underdeveloped or vise versa your pelvis will be pulled out of its proper position and the result will be a domino effect of muscular strain and stresses that radiates from your pelvis to the top of your head and down to the tips of your toes.

So, when you get a chance, go online or *gasp* to the library and find yourself an anatomical muscular system chart and take a good long look it. Note how the layers of muscle fibers run for each level and you'll have a greater understanding of how they all work in concert to give the body its phenomenal ability to move on almost every conceivable plane.

Now when it comes to working the butt muscles, this is one area where you can work a little more deeply, either with a loose fist or the heel of your hand. The important thing to remember is to keep your work on the actual muscles between the borders delineated by the femur on the most lateral aspect, and the sacrum on the medial aspect.

Because of the varying angles of the muscles here a nice way to start is with a loose fist. At the base of the cheek, near the sits bones gently roll with a little lift, upwards. This is one of those moments when just thinking about a little lift will manifest it immediately. So, with your loose fist at the base of the cheek and your free hand flat at the top of it, thoughtfully push that bulk of muscle upward into the cup of the flat hand and roll it downward again with an easy rhythm. This can be done both in increments up and down the whole of the cheek as well as from the medial (inside) border to the lateral one making sure to try and work the muscle as completely as possible while being mindful about not putting pressure directly on any bony prominences. You'll know you're on a bony prominence when you hear, "Ow".

Whenever you're working on the body from the pelvis to the toes, whenever possible use upward strokes. This is because of the valves in the leg veins and their angle. The body works hard enough to return blood to the heart from the feet so rather than pushing the blood back down, the object is to help the body, so keep your stroking either side to side or from the bottom up.

Now there are some folks who are just solid as a rock down here, and not from working out, just because of tension. Or maybe your partner just can't relax and let go, I mean let's face it, in all reality we're programmed to be a little nervous about what's going to happen when someone touches our butt, even in a non-sexual sense. If that is the case and your partner just can't let go, it's your job to respect that and not force the issue.

Tummy Rubbing

(Just a quick word cause we're actually still working on the posterior part of the body)

There are stabilizing pelvic muscles that can only be reached through the anterior (front) of the body, including some of the hip flexors but we're going to leave those to the professionals.

As for tummy rubbing, if that's something your partner is okay with, you can rock left to right with your hands gently curving over the abdominals. You'll want to stay beneath the rib cage and go no further down than the protrusion at the base of the abs. If you wanna shake it up a bit and rub in circles, please be sure to do so but keep it clockwise as that's how stuff moves through the intestinal tract. This can be done easily with the upper body still draped. If you want to use oil you can drape a female's breasts with a towel. Simply have her hold it in place while you slide the sheet out from underneath and secure its upper edge by wedging it with a gentle side to side rocking motion of the hips. The butt will gladly keep the sheet in place.

Okay then, back to the back side and time to move on to the legs.

Legs (Posterior)

Hamstrings and Calf Muscles

Draping: Maintain the draping that you used for the butt. Reapply oil as necessary.

Your hamstrings (affectionately called hammies) are comprised of several different individual muscles bundled together, it's not just one solid slab. Hamstrings originate at the ischial tuberosities of your pelvis (the sits bones), they travel the length of the femur (thigh bone) and attach to the bones of the lower leg (the tibia and the fibula).

When you run, walk, work on the eliptical, bike, blade, skate or basically do anything that's going to get you from Point A to Point B the hamstrings are just one group of muscles called into play. You may notice when you're done with a run that your hammies feel tight and maybe your low back hurts just a bit. Your low back hurts *because* your hammies have tightened up. (No that's not an excuse to stop running or exercising) but it is your cue to learn to stretch properly.

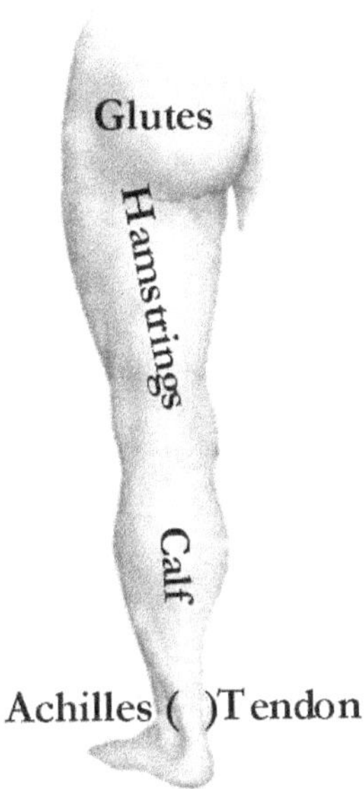

There's a ton of excellent information on proper stretching techniques out there, look for something written at least in part by a Licensed Physical Therapist or Licensed Athletic Trainer. These will be your best sources of sage advice and technique for stretching every part of the body. A caveat, if your source propones 'bouncing' into a stretch, find a different source, that'll just fray your muscle tissue and make you more sore and less able to perform the next time.

Some will espouse stretching before a workout and others won't. Most of the time what they're talking about is a light stretch to get the blood moving to a particular area, then doing a few minutes to warm up a bit before stretching just a little bit more. You don't want to over-stretch before a workout as doing so could destabilize nearby joints.

That having been said, let's get back to massaging the hammies. Warm and spread your oil on the leg starting at the ankle

To get your partner acclimated to your touch in another very sensitive area use a full palm spreading type of touch over the muscles. You know the fibers run length wise down the leg so feel free to move a little laterally too, this will give your partner time to relax and get ready for some real work. Once you sense they've loosened up (you'll be amazed by how quickly you'll be able to determine if they've 'let go' of tension in an area if you're paying attention to them) you can go ahead and start from just above the back of the knee (never directly work the back of the knee, again, leave that to professionals) with a loose fist, hand over hand moving upward toward the glutes. You can even gently round over the hip with your outside hand.

You may sense or feel tight bundles of muscle back there, and if you do, this might be the time to use a little longitudinal (in the direction the muscle fibers run) segmental stretching.

If you sense your partner is loose enough, standing at the side of their leg you can grasp the muscle gently, thumbs closest to your body, give a little lift and gently ease your fingertips over the back of the leg back toward you, then turn so that you're facing their head again and do a little integrative loose fist or flat hand warming.

Once you've finished working the back of the thigh then you can move down to the calf.

EXPECT this area to be sensitive and probably tight.

You want to make sure to thoroughly warm these muscles (Gastrocnemius and Soleus) with firm flat hand or loose fist lengthwise strokes. You will almost certainly feel hard spots and knots, one is almost always near the center of the calf about half way up, another is at a corresponding height on the outer border of the muscles, and the last most common one is on the inner border at the apex of the most round part of the muscle.

If your partner asks you to NOT trigger point these areas please be respectful of that.

The calf muscles respond well to longitudinal muscle stripping, loose fist warming and the same kind of rhythmic kneading you did on the neck.

Alternate these strokes for several minutes feeling free to move up the leg back to the hamstring and even up to the glutes again as you will.

When you're through, using the heel of your hands and starting at the base of the calf, near but not directly on the Achilles Tendon (the heel tendon) lean lightly into the muscle and allow the glide of the oil and your angle to push your hands up the leg, (backing off a bit for the seconds that you're over the back of the knee) and over the hip, perform this two or three times and finish with a feather light fingertip stroke over the length of the area. Release the sheet and re-cover the leg and hip that you just finished before moving on to the other leg. Starting with the proper draping repeat the processes for that particular butt cheek and working your way down the same way again.

Now that we're done with the entire posterior aspect of the body, it's time to have your partner flip so you can work on the front. (Easy now... there's going to be a happy chappy for romantic partners in just a little bit but for now... let's keep it clean shall we?)

The Front of the Body

From the Bottom up

Draping: Once again you're going to expose your first leg of choice up to the hip, anchoring the sheet this time under the butt and the opposite leg.

Again you're going to warm and spread your oil from the foot up to the hip. It's okay to get the inner thigh as long as you respect the boundaries of your partner. This isn't the time to get goofy or try to push boundaries. The fact is as we all know the thigh is extremely sensitive to touch and its inner aspect is definitely considered an erogenous zone. One of the best ways to ensure that your intent to nurture is NOT misconstrued as any kind of sexual touch is to imagine that your partner is wearing shorts and NOT work beyond where the fabric would fall. This is also the time to make sure that your intent and your touch are in harmony.

-        Make sure that your touch is firm rather than feather light or in any way able to be construed as teasing.

-        Keep both hands on the leg so that your partner knows where each one is at all times.

-        Fix your intent in your own mind and it will be communicated through your hands.

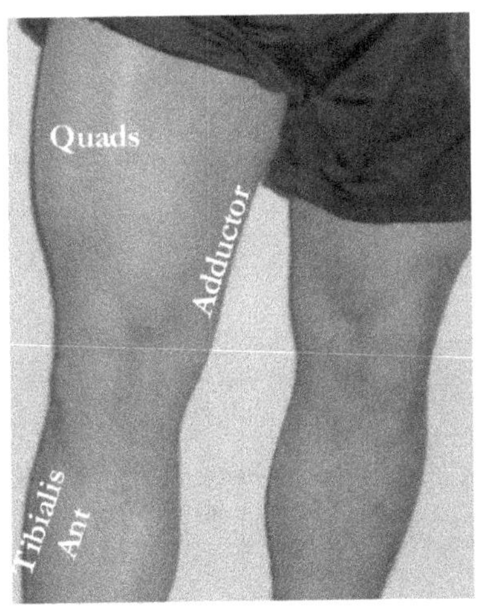

The thigh (quadriceps) is sensitive and a very common place to carry tension. It's also a very difficult group of muscles to stretch effectively without compromising other joints much in the way the hurdler's stretch compromises the knee. Keeping this in mind it's best to use a flat hand or heel of the hand technique with firm but not deep pressure. It won't be uncommon for some of your massage partners to have a very dramatic reaction to having this part of their body worked. (We'll get into the possibility of emotional release in a little bit).

You can try to do a little palm style lateral spreading (these muscle fibers run longitudinally too, just like our dear hammies), but you're probably going to have better success if you stick to light thumb over thumb muscle stripping and flat handed warming techniques (all done longitudinally of course).

By now you should be noticing that you're feeling a lot more comfortable with your ability to sense how your partner is responding to what you're doing but remember, both of you, that we have verbal communication for a reason. Like any other tool, it's there, so use it.

Check in with your partner, "how's that? Is it too much? Do you want more pressure?"

Likewise if you're on the receiving end and you want your partner to lean on a knot or a trigger point, guide them to the spot, "a little up... toward the spine... no down... ahhh there..." take a couple breaths, and if the area releases you may find that suddenly that amount of pressure hurts instead of feeling good so you must tell your partner, "...ahhh that's good, you can let go now..." or some obvious but gentle cue to let them know what they're doing is working for you.

Okay... sorry about the digression there, back to the legs.

Now that you've finished with the front of the thigh, you can move down to the tibialis anterior, it's that long slender muscle on the outside of the shin bone. This one is perfect for a little bit of thumb over thumb stripping, and maybe even a little lateral spreading by using the thumb. It's a very tender muscle so you don't want to use more than fingertip pressure on it.

From there you can work your way around the ankle, small circles around those knobs of bone on the inside and the outside feel really good!

On the top of the foot you can feel the long bones (metatarsals) there so feel free to use your fingers lightly between them, much like you did for the ribs and the intercostals. If you can feel each metatarsal individually, (usually at the base of each respective toe) you can grasp it at the front and back (or from the top of the foot and the underside) and give it a little jostle independent of the others, it's a very subtle movement that you might not even feel as the giver, but your recipient will feel it. Now go ahead and say 'hello' to each metatarsal and each toe in turn.

When you're done with the top of the foot it's time to move on to the plantar surface (the bottom of your foot). Web your fingers together and wrap them around the top of the foot while placing your thumbs against the arch of the foot on the underside. Now using your thumbs spread the bottom of the foot like you were spreading a pizza dough. (Be careful not to put tension on the top of the foot and thereby on the ankle, your fingers are just there to give you a little anchoring.)

You can use a loose fist up and down the plantar surface, and use fingertip circles around the border of the heel.

When you're through with the foot a little jostle or gentle rolling of it between your hands is a nice comfortable finishing move.

After that, a simple palm or flat hand run back up the leg from the foot to the hip integrates the limb back into the whole. Cover leg and move on to the other repeating the process.

Anterior Arms and Pectorals

Draping: Secure sheet around your partner's torso slightly lower than the arm pits, both arms should be out from under the sheet and the upper chest should be exposed. If your partner is a male and he's comfortable with it, you may secure the sheet around his waist. If your partner is female you'll be working the pecs outside of the sheet since they are higher up on the chest than the boobs are, but you'll most likely do any tummy rubbing through the sheet (if she wants it at all, definitely ask before touching).

On the chest a little oil goes a long way (unless we're talking about hairy chests, then you'll need more).

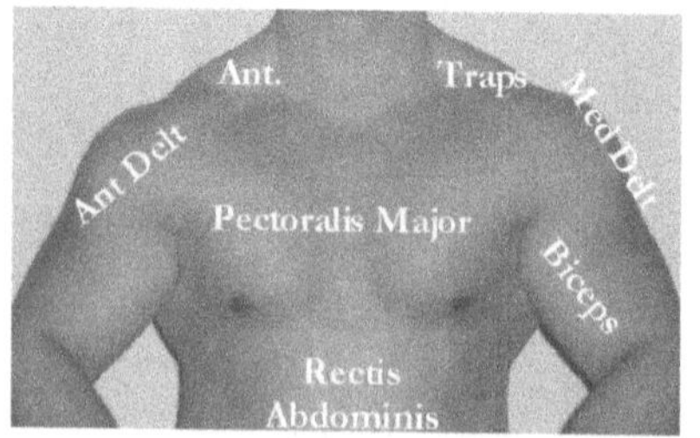

Handle the anterior of the arms almost identically to the posterior with two handed kneading, a little light stripping and some flat hand warming that you carry very gently over the front of the shoulder.

A little traction at the fingers is nice and a good way to get your partner's shoulders out of their ears, watch as you're providing the traction, (you'll see what I mean).

When you get to the pecs however, be gentle, these muscles are tender and very sensitive and are unaccustomed to touch. The pecs lay horizontally across the chest, in some folks this is going to be very easy to see, and in others not so much, there is a faint angle to them but for your intentions here you just need to know that they're horizontal. Longitudinal spreading, and light fingertip kneading at the lateral border of pecs can be a great relief for anyone who drives long distances, types a lot or spends an inordinate amount of time with their hands in front of them.

This is another group of muscles that are grossly under stretched so while you're looking up how to stretch your hammies and quads properly, check out pec stretches too.

An easy one is the doorway stretch. Standing in the doorway, raise one arm up to either shoulder height or just below (don't raise it higher than shoulder level). Brace the arm with the doorjamb and gently turn away until you feel a comfortable stretch in the chest and anterior shoulder. Hold for 10 seconds and repeat 3 times then change sides.

Always stretch bilaterally (both sides). Too often we focus on whichever side is bothering us, ignoring the other side only to find some time later that we're faced with the same pains there. Most often it's because we didn't treat both sides at the same time.

To finalize pec/anterior arm work, you can start from the head of the table and simply glide your hands across each pectoralis muscle and down that arm, then circle back up to the shoulders and around to the back of the neck.

If you wish at this point to do a little more neck work, please do feel free to do so, but if not and depending on whether your partner wants tummy rubbing you might even be done. If you're not done, then...

The Tummy

(Yes, just a little more)

Draping: For male partners it's generally accepted to make sure the sheet is secured at hip level. But for women you can either anchor the sheet under their arms or under the ribs on either side by slipping it beneath them while gently rocking the body.

This can be one of the most ticklish places as we all know, and we do have a tendency to guard it, (that just means tightening it up). Keeping that in mind this is a place where you might want to exercise sincerity and care.

Standing at your partner's side introduce your touch by gently laying your open hands in the center of the belly. From this position you can feel the rectus abdominus (the abs), and may want to rock your partner back and forth for about 15 to 30 seconds.

After your partner has relaxed into your touch you can start to work in small clockwise circles moving concentrically outward from the area of the belly button out to the edges of the abdomen, and then back inside. Always keep your circles moving in a clockwise direction whether they're smaller and tighter ones around the border or broad and light over the whole of the abs. This is because of how waste moves through the intestinal tract.

Once you're at the edges of the abdomen you can work the border in smaller circles. Always start working the outer edges at the recipient's lower right hand side, keep your fingertip pressure firm but your fingers themselves relaxed. Work your way up the side of the abdominal cavity to the base of the ribs, across the upper border, and down the left hand side finishing the set with a couple full belly clockwise motions, maybe a little criss crossing before a light easy release.

And there you have it, you've just given your first 'whole body massage'. The time it takes, anywhere from forty minutes to an hour is up to you and your partner and the prospect of reciprocity.

All the aforementioned having been said, you have your own rhythms, your own comfortable and innate motions. Sometimes you'll be inclined to rub an area in a circular motion, that's great, do it. When your thumbs start to hurt go ahead and slide into one of the other styles here, whether 'fingertip group', loose fist, heel of the hand, whatever's going to work between you and your partner.

Touching is instinctive, obey yours and honor your partner's, all else will come as it should, with patience and practice.

Emotional Release

Our bodies are our houses, they're where we live no matter where we go, and we do accumulate a lot of stuff. Sometimes because of prior experiences and body issues we've held over the years we develop certain holding patterns.

A boy who shot up further and faster than his peers in school may develop sensitivity in his pectorals (chest muscles) because he slouched to hide his growth or to fit in better. Maybe even because he was taunted as a 'bean pole' when everyone else was just shrimps.

A woman might be particularly reluctant to let her legs or butt relax if she's been self conscious about it because perhaps hers is a little larger or a little more round. Let's face it, Sir Mix-A-Lot and his adoration of a nice round rump can rarely fix the trauma of school age taunts such as, 'bubble butt and fatass', (though the well rounded rumps of the world do get the last laugh... in the end).

So, the possibility exists that when you're working on an area in which there is some psychologically originated sensitivity (upper thighs and butt for a victim of sexual abuse for instance), that your partner may wind up with an emotional response.

The response could be anything from fear to tears to seemingly sudden crankiness depending on the severity of the issue.

It's up to the two of you to communicate about it. You don't have to know everything and they don't have to tell you everything. But your partner does need to tell you to stop if that's what they want. And You have a duty to respect them and stop, and if you're up for it, let them know you're there and willing to listen if they want to talk.

Chapter 6

Working on Friends and Family

There are some special issues and challenges that you'll be faced with when it comes to working on friends and family members.

The first one is boundaries.

You're going to have to decide together if your partner is going to keep their clothes on, if you're going to use oil, what areas to work on and what areas they might not be comfortable with you touching. But don't let this deter you.

This is yet another area where communication is the beginning of this stage in your newly changing relationship. Honest, non-judgmental communication is the foundation on which this new aspect of your relationship will be built.

Now of course you're not going to be offering massages of any type or stripe to that family member, family 'friend', or anyone who has either behaved in a sexually inappropriate way or even made you feel uncomfortable "In

That Way" (and let's face it we all know that feeling, it's just one of the many instincts we're graced with to keep us safe). If they're not someone you feel comfortable being alone with, and not someone you can trust when you're alone with them in a closed room, you don't want to work on that person and you have every right to say "No" or not offer at all. Giving a massage is a chance to connect with and nurture your own spirit, and it should be a loving experience just as receiving one should be, and for that there has to be a sense of safety and trust.

Okay, now that we're clear on that we can move forward knowing that the only people on and with whom you'll be working are those you feel safe with, and who feel safe with you.

So then, one of the most difficult things to get past is the social taboo of skin to skin touch, especially with family. Any massage therapist, in the course of obtaining their training, has had to work to overcome some level of shyness, social taboo, and the idea of acceptable non-sexual touch from gender to gender.

Personally, I came into massage through nature. As a child I was always one of those 'touchy-feely' ones. Mom came home from a hard days' work and her feet were killing her, I'd rub 'em. After holiday dinners, as soon as I was big enough to reach their shoulders while they were seated, when the whole family was just finishing up their meals I'd start around the table with post meal neck rubs, (hey it got me excused from the table sooner). It eventually became something that my family members looked forward to.

In second grade I had a teacher who had horrible upper back and neck problems so when it came time for Reading she would sit in her chair, call on me (usually as one of the first to read a page or two), then ask for me to rub her neck and shoulders when I was done. Keep in mind here this was during the seventies, times were a lot different and there was no reason to fear innocent physical contact. The fact was, she hurt and somehow discovered that I could make that hurt ease up a bit. I'm not sure it ever occurred to me to say no.

The point is that just because I started exercising this 'nurturing touch' somewhere near the age of about six or seven, doesn't mean that it's a gift for just a few people. It's human nature to touch and be touched, to seek out contact and connection with other people. I just wasn't shy about it.

That being said, by the time I went to massage school and we had to get our hands on practice with friends and family, I gotta say it was pretty darned awkward, at least for me, to get my septuagenarian grandmother or great aunt pretty much naked under a sheet and work on them like they were folks I didn't know. I don't know whether it was awkward for them either. It might very well have been but I know it would have been worse if we didn't already have the 'holiday dinner backrub' history. But, that is exactly why it's important to talk about expectations, about those boundaries and to do what you can to make sure that both of you feel as comfortable as possible.

Embarrassing Moments On The Table

From flatulence to the unintentional erection these moments may happen.

Say you're working on grandma or grandpa and he or she let's one rip while you're working on their back or while they're rolling over or whatever, follow their lead. Sometimes an older folk may not even realize that they broke wind, so follow their lead. If they say excuse me, a simple "no problem" or "More room out than in" usually sets them at ease and de-fuses their embarrassment. But I warn you... however you and your partner react... whatever you do, Don't Sniff!

As for erections, partials or even a chubby stub; if your partner is someone with whom you are NOT sexual, like a grandfather, uncle, brother, next door neighbor, and as long as you're not getting a lecherous vibe from them (which you wouldn't cause you're not gonna put yourself into that position by working on anyone who gives you that vibe anyway right? Right.) then try to understand they're probably more embarrassed than you are. So the easiest way to get their mind off it is to simply continue as if it's not there. So you're dancing around the white elephant in the room for a few minutes, its okay. It's most likely the result of some long draining strokes up the posterior of the legs, the blood has to go somewhere so don't worry. It will go away, just carry on your conversation (if you're having one) and don't poke it. Also don't get disturbed if they try to rearrange their 'junk', the odds are they're just trying to get it under control.

Doing massages on friends and family gives you an opportunity to be a partner in their health and wellness. If you work on each other regularly you can keep tabs on everything from skin discoloration and texture to moles (watch for changing borders or growth, and if noted strongly suggest to your partner that they go see a dermatologist or have their doctor look at it.) You're not a doctor, or a diagnostician but you are going to be able to objectively note changes in skin tone, elasticity, again moles, sebaceous cysts etc. especially on the back, neck and shoulders. It's the same concept as a husband or romantic partner being more likely to discover lumps in their girlfriend's breasts than she is.

If you do encounter something unusual in the texture or appearance of your partner's skin the first thing to do is DON'T PANIC and most certainly Don't Panic THEM. More often than not you'll find that your partner is already aware of certain incongruities, lumps, bruises, fatty deposits, moles etc. So as a caring individual it's your job to simply ask them if they're aware that something exists at a particular place on their landscape and take it from there. Depending on how extreme the incongruity is you may simply want to suggest that they have their doctor check it out next time they go.

Of course if there are breaks in the skin, weeping from a wound, exudate that's green or yellow in color and has a distinctly unhealthy aroma then you might want to suggest a special visit to a licensed health care provider sooner rather than later.

With family in particular, there are times when well meaning relatives may wind up putting you in an awkward situation by offering you money.

You're NOT a professional, morally and ethically you can not accept it for performing a massage.

Chapter 7 – You and Your Partner

Massage, Sex, and the big 'O'

This chapter is all about sex, pretty much humanity's favorite pass time (no matter what MLB would have us believe), and how to apply what you've learned about your partner and yourself so far. Also, a word on what works in the bedroom and what doesn't.

That last one is simple, what works in the bedroom is anything you're both (or all) amenable to; from the wonderful standard of Missionary position, to Bondage, Discipline, Domination, Submission, Sado-Masochism, Fetish play, man or chickwiching, filming/webcams online posting, (if you're going to go this route please make sure you're posting your material on a server that at least makes an attempt to shield surfing children from pornography. And if you're filming with the pretext of keeping it just for the entertainment of the participants then you might as well not even bother filming it because what you least want the world to see will somehow make it out there online; you may be the next "model and rockstar"), other than that there's very little that's not acceptable between two or more consenting and well informed adults. Of course if you are playing in a larger group it's not enough to just buy the econo-pack of condoms (try the ribbed ones or the studded ones) but you actually have to **use** them. For women, go ahead and get a few female condoms, give the guys a break. Also make sure you have plenty of water based spermicidal lubricant around (anything with an oil base can break down the latex of a condom). The point is, BE SAFE.

What DOESN'T work is anything that involves an unwilling or underage party.

Now here's something that may or may not blow your mind depending on how much you really know the opposite gender. As behaviorally different as we've been programmed to be. When it comes to erogenous zones and the nerve clusters that can drive each of us to distraction, many of them are almost identical.

Men	**Women**
Neck	Neck
Nipples	Nipples
Lower Abs	Lower Abs
Inner Thigh	Inner Thigh
Perineum	Perineum
Penis	Clitoris
Anus	Anus
Scrotum	Labia

And there's plenty more but discovery is half the fun and don't forget, for all the similarities there are many spots that are unique to each individual.

What REALLY Constitutes Sex?

There's a disturbing concept among teens these days that sex strictly means penetration of the vagina by a penis.

This IS WRONG!

Girls are sometimes coerced into giving guys blow jobs because the guys tell them that it's not sex. This is BULLSHIT. Any activity that centers around genital stimulation *of* either party for the purpose of pleasure or orgasm *by* either party IS sex.

Whether it's vaginal penetration, anal penetration, a girl giving a blow job, or a boy munching on a muffin, (hello what part of oral SEX doesn't say SEX?) if it pertains to genital stimulation for the purpose of pleasure or orgasm it IS sex. (Yes I said it twice, but only because it bore repeating.).

If you don't have the maturity to be honest with yourself and your partner about what you're doing and why, then boys stick with spanking the monkey, and girls get happily acquainted with all ten of your fingers, that's one of the reasons we have so many. Okay preaching's over.

Your Brain as your Orgasm Organ

While there is no doubt that genital stimulation is the catalyst for orgasm, the truth is that the orgasm starts and ends in the brain. It's true. Think about it, if you're stressed, if you're preoccupied with a to-do list the length of your...um...arm, it's going to be a lot harder to convince yourself to let go and dive head first into that beautiful oblivion of orgasmic bliss no matter *what* part of your physical body is being stimulated, or how.

** A note about erectile facilitators (i.e. erection making pharmaceuticals) These drugs work by forcing the body's vessels and major vascularities to relax so the penis can then become more readily engorged with blood enabling it to become erect. The human body should NOT require drugs of this nature to be used daily. Guys, if you can't get it up or keep it up, there's obviously a reason whether physiological or psychological. Please Please Please, for yourself, for YOUR enjoyment, for HER or HIS enjoyment and for those who love you... look for the root CAUSE rather than simply trying to change the state of the symptom.**

Sex is meant to be rapturous, otherwise why would we get such rapturous enjoyment out of it?

One of the best ways to ensure that you get the most out of any sexual experience is to honor yourself. I'm not talking about getting yourself off first, I'm not talking about making sure to please your partner and leave your own needs out in the cold, (that's called sacrifice and it's NOT healthy).

The kind of honoring I'm talking about here is different, it comes with knowing who you are, what turns you on, what your limits are, what your likes and dislikes are or exploring these ideas while feeling safe in your sexual environment. Again, these things can mean different things to different people.

Where one person's honesty and honor might lie in the fulfillment of a fetishist fantasy with a willing and respectful partner, another's might lie in coming clean with their partner about the fact that they don't like doggy style. Point is, it's all very personal and just as individual as we are from one another.

If you and your partner or partners are already open and supportive enough to be able to communicate fetish, role playing scenarios, B&D/S&M desires and needs to one another then this next part probably won't even begin to stir you.

If however you are like a huge majority of human beings who are still repressed inside after having spent a lifetime being inundated with other people's puritanical beliefs that sex is something used only for reproduction, or that masturbation is dirty or evil or something you never let your lover know you do, and for all your verbal openness still cringe inside when any conversation veers toward sex or sexual fulfillment; then the following might be a great way to open yourself up mentally, yes physically but even more importantly, emotionally.

Warming Up

Like when you exercise, sex often needs a 'warm up' period too. It's called foreplay and it's an art (for both genders).

First facts:

1. Sex doesn't look as pretty in real life as it does in the movies and on tv.

2. Sex can be noisy, and I don't mean just the moaning and groaning. (ever heard of a queef?). Oh yeah speaking of moaning and groaning... it's more like panting and grunting peppered with the occasional word of encouragement more often than not. (Let's face it, it takes focus to have an orgasm AND to bring one to your partner!)

3. Belly smacking happens, things jiggle and shake and boobs slide off to the sides (well real ones do anyway) so learn to love it, admire it and cherish it then get ON with the fun.

4. People DO get tired and collapse before they come. (Just one more reason to cuddle and foreplay a little longer then try again later).

5. Sex IS MESSY, sometimes clumsy, and very often juicy. And depending on the toys, lubes and sauces you bring to bed with you, you might have a heckuva mess to clean up or shower off in the morning so make sure you leave plenty of time to get that butterscotch all gone.

For women, foreplay usually begins with kissing and cuddling. As a rule we LOVE to kiss and be kissed. If you're a guy whose not big into kissing, think about this... kissing is the first step in getting girls hot and the hotter your girl gets, the more likely she is to slide those lips of hers right down the glory line to that attention craving 'junior' of yours.

Where do we like to kiss and be kissed (before the clothes come off?)? Lips, earlobes (that little spot just under and behind the ear lobe is a HUGE hot spot for women), neck (pretty much anywhere on the neck but the more toward the back the more intense the turn on [and no hickies please, a nip here and there is awesome but unless you're Dracula keep the sucking to small puckery patches that aren't meant to brand us and we'll do the same for you... if that's what you want.]).

Women also love the firm but tentative hand slide up the shirt, it tells us you want more but are waiting for permission (now *that* is consideration).

A sexually savvy guy will pay a lot of attention to the way his woman touches him, if she traces his lines with feather soft strokes and swirls then the odds are that is how she likes to be touched as well. That kind of touch will allow her a deeper initial relaxation, which equates to deeper comfort level and much deeper satisfaction for both parties when the end has come and gone. (Girls, pay attention here too, cause men do the same thing. They touch *us* like *they* like to be touched as well. Except for the whole nipples as radio dials thing... where *did* you guys get that?)

Now I'm not sure what exactly boys are taught when they're introduced into the seamy steamy world of fiery male sexuality, but through the shared experiences of many, it's a rare man who has been taught to take his cues from the woman. Same for us guys, girls aren't taught anything about the communication of pre-sex touch.

If you can't quite get what I'm saying, or worse yet, don't believe it, think about the following.

Think about the Board Room Executive who spends all day making decisions, bearing the burden of control and command who then comes home to his wife and grabs her tight, dominating her toward the bedroom where he captures her to his needs. Now unless that is really his personality through and through (you might be surprised to find that some of these folks with corporate power, be they male or female actually have a greater need to be allowed to hand over control to someone they trust in the bedroom), have you as the lover, wife or partner ever considered that maybe he's trying to clue you in? That maybe he's trying to show you how he wants YOU to make love with him? Surprise the heck out of him one day and ask him. (Also understand that he might not even realize that part of him wants this.) Of course if you're not comfortable vocalizing, twine your fingers into the hair at the base of his neck, gently but firmly grasping a handful of it and pull his lips away from yours, look him dead in the eye and take control without saying a word. Maybe deny him a kiss while smiling coyly at him, see what his reaction is. Gently turn his head away from yours and lip his earlobe and when *you're* ready, urge *him* into the bedroom, living room, kitchen, den, wherever.

If this is your first time trying to take control, tread lightly until you're both sure you want it this way, this time. As adults we forget to play, so take this time and just have fun with each other. Give yourselves that permission.

The signals you get from tiny little experiments like these will give you deeper insight into what he or she wants and sometimes needs and is guaranteed to bring another dimension to your sex life that could well ripple out into the whole of your relationship.

Sexual needs and desires are fluid. One day you may need to be submissive, the next day you may need to feel dominant but no matter the style of the encounter the equal fulfillment of each other's needs is the most important thing.

Bodies, Yours And Your Partner's

Everyone loves to feel that their body is being appreciated.

Men's erogenous zones are just as sensitive (sometimes moreso) than womens' and strangely enough they are almost in the same locations as ours.

Stroke his chest, the outer edges of his pectorals as you take his shirt off and don't be afraid to go for the nipple, brush it with your thumb and note his reaction (a shy gasp of surprise never sounded so erotic).

Let the back of your hand trail down his abs and revel in the little quake you feel underneath as you head toward the waistband of his pants. (Men take notes here you can do the same to women and we love it!).

Take the time to explore and discover your lover's nooks and crannies, or if you already know them, play them.

Also, while you're unwrapping each other like Christmas presents, if there's a part of your erogenous landscape that you've never shared with your partner and you really want to, a gently guided hand, yours over his or hers (try starting this without a word) can open up whole new levels of enjoyment.

Often when it comes to introducing something new to a sexual relationship there is hesitance and uncertainty on both parts. The one who is initiating the new scenario may very well be frightened of turning their partner off, of being ridiculed for having the desire or even the desire to experiment.

Such is the case with anal play for instance. The area around the anus is filled with nerves and is an extraordinarily sensitive erogenous zone. It should be approached with consideration whether it's a simple caress in the general vicinity that's desired, or if it's actual penetration whether digital or penile, or with toys. The fact is it's not easy to indicate to a partner that you've always been curious about adding that area to the playground if it's not already on the menu, no matter how you want to experiment.

So sensitivity, trust and open mindedness are essential in this regard. Also the partner asking for the experiment has to understand that it's possible their partner might not be ready for it. Hopefully you know your consented limitations and you know enough about each other to be able to broach such subjects openly and without judgement.

Now That You're Both Nekked

Let the stroking begin.

A great way to start is with this encounters' first recipient on their stomach. Usually this is the female (let's face it there's little more that's mood making, or more erotic than your partner's sensitive hands exploring your landscape without hesitance or shame) so guys, warm up a dollop of your fave massage oil between those big beautiful mitts of yours, get situated at the foot of the bed, couch, floor... wherever; rest your hands at your partner's heels (one hand to each), lean forward and luge your way up those legs!

Your thumbs should be on the inner part of the back of the legs as you reach your partner's butt, this helps you keep your motions under control and helps prevent too fast a slide that can result in unintended or painful slip.

With relaxed semi-splayed fingers go ahead and cruise on up those cheeks, maybe making small circles or half circles as you work your way up first around the hip bone, over the crest of the hip and into the small of the back. Once you're in the small of the back you can use your thumbs to circle or strip up the sides of the spine a little ways then draw your hands back down lightly to where you started and repeat the process (as many times as you and your partner want).

When you're ready to move on up to the back as a whole feel free to find a comfortable straddling position and continue.

By now you should have a very thorough knowledge of how your partner likes to be massaged. The main difference between giving them an erotic massage or a platonic massage is INTENT.

Platonic intent is actually reinforced by proper draping techniques which provide definite boundaries that are agreed upon by both parties.

Since this isn't a sex manual I'm going to leave the refining of these particular techniques to you and move on to the next segment.

Accessories

Safety First:

The first safety device you'll need are condoms. They come in a variety of sizes and styles. There are condoms for males and condoms for females. Some are ribbed, some are studded. They usually have expiration dates on them so either use them before hand or take your chances afterwards (personally I'd suggest getting a fresh batch if yours are expired).

The second thing you'll need is water based spermicidal lubricant. There are lots of excellent ones out on the market, just take a peek at prime time (cable) television to find the latest innovations. KY is *the* most well known brand of lubricant, but there are lots of others out there too, don't be afraid to give 'em a try to see what you like. Just remember they should: 1. be water based, and 2. contain spermicide, (unless you're trying to get pregnant then scratch all that).

The next safety device may not apply to everyone, but definitely does to those who are into games. You'll need a

'Safe*word*' just in case the games get to be too much. That is a word that indicates you're serious about stopping whatever's going on, usually it's something used during BDSM play.

Toys

Whatever your pleasure, fetish or curiosity is there are a huge quantity of places to purchase the necessary accoutrements both on line and in the 'real world'.

If you and your partner are moving into experimentation with either devices or techniques or both, you have the means at your disposal to research and learn some basic terminology as well as whatever tools and toys may be employed. It's almost guaranteed that if you have a fetish or a desire, there's someone else out there too who's either been there, or done that and is happy to share their experiences and divest their knowledge to you.

For beginners I would strongly suggest heading out into the real world to your local intimates shop, usually stores that specialize in intimate apparel or novelty gifts, as well as head shops (if there are still any in existence) have a section devoted to sexual play.

Often the sales people are knowledgeable and more than willing to welcome newcomers into a new dimension of joy. Of course if you're on the shy side you can do a little internet research first to acquaint yourself with particular terms and get familiar with the sight of some of the toys you might be interested in checking out.

If you do choose to start with an online community do yourself a favor and make sure to research it thoroughly. Lurk on the boards, get a feel for how the members treat themselves and each other, participate in a few conversations but never never give out personal information over the internet (even though we all already know not to do that).

In Conclusion:

It is a sad fact of today's society that because of a few 'bad apples' we've become afraid to touch one another at all, let alone in a positive and constructive way. We are inherently a social species that has become physically isolative, and without the nurturing influence of positive touch it is conceivable that our very humanity could be in jeopardy. It starts with our children, why is it that violence is a more acceptable outlet than a hug?

What needs to be taught to our children, best through our own example, is not to *refrain* from contact, but how to *accept* or *reject* contact at the appropriate times and in the appropriate ways.

To touch someone is natural, whether it is a good thing or a bad thing depends entirely on the INTENT. Too many people in today's world are afraid to touch or be touched for all the wrong reasons. They're afraid that someone will misconstrue a gentle hand given in comfort as a sexual gesture, or a pass because instead of having the strength of character to turn around and simply ask, "Please don't touch me," an unwilling recipient will hiss something about "Sexual Harrassment!"

I would like to know why, in our world today it is more acceptable for a violent act to be perpetrated than for a hug to be given.

Children are not allowed to hug one another in school? Nor to hug a teacher? Good lord my teachers would've been terrified had the world been like this when I was a child! I thought the world of most of my teachers (despite the whole homework and not doing it thing) and the most natural expression of that affection and respect for them was at the end of the year to give them a hug goodbye!

The sooner we learn the difference between touching someone out of simple human fellow-feeling, and unwanted sexual advances the sooner we can safely return to nurturing ourselves, our families, friends and children.

Sexual harassment has less to do with sex than it does with a lack of respect, just as the crime of rape has almost nothing to do with sex and instead is about the exercise of power of some kind over another person.

The sooner we learn how to live the example of respect and nurturing intent for ourselves and those around us, the sooner the ripple effect can spread and we can return to the understanding that people are stronger together than we will ever be able to be when kept separate from one another.

Author Bio:

Jill A. Carlton is an Author, licensed Massage Therapist and Radiographic Technologist with almost 18 years experience in alternative and mainstream health care.

She has spent the majority of that time working with individuals and couples, teaching nurturing touch. She is currently spending most of her time working as a speaker and a Life Balance Assistant and Positivity trainer.

Other Works by J. A. Carlton

Fiction:

Broken
Wednesday's Child
Into The Fire
Heroes of the Line; Nick, of Time

Coming soon:

Fortune's Tide.

Non-Fiction:

Touch Me – A Beginner's Guide to Massage

Coming soon:

At The Crossroads – The Destiny of Choice

148